HEARTWOOD

The Walt McDonald First-Book Poetry Series

HEARTWOOD

Miriam Vermilya

To Michael,
the Greenville Poets
Myrna Stone
Cathy Essinger

Catskill Poetry Workshop 2003

Texas Tech University Press

The Walt McDonald First-Book Poetry Series

Robert Fink, Series Editor

This book was set in Garamond and Papyrus. The paper used in this book meets the minimum requirements of ANSI/NISO Z39.48-1992 (R1997).∞

Design by Tamara Kruciak

Printed in the United States of America

Library of Congress Cataloging-in-Publication Data
    Vermilya, Miriam,
        Heartwood / Miriam Vermilya.
            p. cm. — (The Walt McDonald first-book poetry series)
        ISBN 0-89672-421-X (cloth : alk. paper)
            I. Title. II. Series.
    PS3572.E665 H4 2000
    811'.6—dc21
                                                                99-087736

00 01 02 03 04 05 06 07 08 / 9 8 7 6 5 4 3 2 1

Texas Tech University Press
Box 41037
Lubbock, Texas 79409-1037 USA
800-832-4042
ttup@ttu.edu
Http://www.ttup.ttu.edu

For Jack, Michael, and Joanne

Acknowledgments

Grateful acknowledgment is made to the editors of the
following publications, in which a number of these poems
first appeared (some in earlier versions), or are forthcoming:

Baltimore Review: "Another Season"
Buffalo Spree: "Love," "Ode to Schultz Motors"
Cedar Hill Review: "My Cousin Charlotte, Dancing," "Nitro,"
    "Summerfield's Steakhouse, Detroit"
Circumference: "Le Déjeuner sur l'Herbe," "Patchwork,"
    "Remembering the Horses"
Monocacy Valley Review: "Windows"
The New England Review: "Heartwood"
The New Renaissance: "Reclamation," "Ten Items or Less" (as
    "Kroger's, Four PM"), and (forthcoming in Vol. 12)
    "Performance Art," "Pressure," "Wa'hela Tells Her Side,"
    "In November, " "Leaving"
Poetpourri: "Unredeemed," "Will the Last One to Leave Please
    Turn Out the Lights?"
Poetry: "Consider Socrates," "Ephemeroptera," "Heart and
    Soul"
Red Rock Review: "The Nearsighted"
The Sow's Ear: "Naming the Birds"
Talking River Review: "The Hospitality of Chairs"
Weber Studies: "On Hearing of the Death of a Friend,"
    "Washing the Clothes of the Dead," "When the Second
    Chance Cloning Clinic Opens"
Writer's Journal: "Kites"

The Greenville Poets wish to express their gratitude and thanks
    to Robert Fink and Judith Keeling of Texas Tech University
    Press for their belief in this manuscript. Without their
    continued support this book would not have been possible.

Contents

Introduction

Miriam Vermilya's life's work of poems *Heartwood* is a book which celebrates both the living and the having lived, raising its glass, *"Shalom* to all survivors," to all women gathered around a table, *Shalom* as well to the one who needs to hear a voice calling, *"Darling,"* an invitation to drag her chair across the aisle, join the other women at the table, and "offer up [her] own litany / of loss" ("Summerfield's Steakhouse, Detroit").

Heartwood is a summing-up, the book's persona putting her house in order ("In November" and "Consider Socrates"), reclaiming what is lost, steadfastly refusing to let love fall away. Hers is "the beat of a faithful heart" ("Houses"). She shares her wry, comic look back at family, friends, marriage, at a life contained by art, music, and poetry. Her comic stance is a kind of gallows humor, an almost sardonic confession seeking some assurance of redemption, making a final expiation before joining the ranks of the "tidy, / blameless dead" ("Consider Socrates").

In his poem "Under Ben Bulben," William Butler Yeats instructs his fellow poets to "learn your trade. / Sing whatever is well made." *Heartwood* reveals a poet who has indeed learned her trade. This collection of "well made" poems also reflects Yeats's final admonition to poets: "Cast a cold eye / On life, on death. / Horseman, pass by!" ("Under Ben Bulben"). Miriam Vermilya's eye is not an indifferent, unfeeling one; it is the objective eye that Yeats knew memorable poets must possess. This is not to say there is no passion, no fire reflected in this look, but the eye seems mostly that of a close observer, a sentient, sensuous being who is looking back over her life and attempting to tidy up by casting Yeats's "cold" eye on the lives and the deaths of friends and family. She also seems to have a premonition of her own death as she anticipates the dark horseman.

The persona's comic stance is the wry one described by Wylie Sypher in his essay "The Meanings of Comedy."

Comedy, Sypher claims, "begins from the absurd and the inexplicable and, like faith, tolerates the miraculous" (Wylie Sypher, ed., *Comedy*, Johns Hopkins University Press, paperback edition, 1980. 238). Sypher contends that "the comic perception comes only when we take a double view—that is, a human view—of ourselves, a perspective by incongruity" *(Comedy* 255). It is appropriate, then, that Miriam Vermilya has chosen "Consider Socrates" as the first poem, an epigraph for the sequence to follow. Socrates, according to Sypher, insisted that "anyone who can write tragedy can also write comedy" *(Comedy* 215). Sypher explains that Socrates was the "proper one to hold this notion" because he was "comedian and martyr, mocker and moralist" *(Comedy* 215). Students of *Heartwood* will discover the same can be said of Miriam Vermilya and her book's autobiographical persona. The opening poem could be titled "Consider Vermilya," as she casts her cold eye on her life and foreshadowed death, and lifts with Socrates the cup of hemlock, a toast to the horseman who will not stop for them before they've sorted through their "aphorisms, taking / care to jettison any less-than- / cogent thoughts," putting their house in order ("Consider Socrates").

Section I begins the summing-up, the persona's looking back at what has been lost as she sings for those who have passed and are passing. It is her attempt at reclaiming the lost—her family and friends—or, if there is no other choice, to try and replace them. Here begins a kind of expiation for somehow having sinned against, having failed, family and friends. When the persona is called to climb up behind the horseman and join the dead, she wants to be "tidy / blameless" ("Consider Socrates"), forgiven.

"Houses" is the first poem in Section I and introduces the persona's quest to reclaim her family, the homes where she "celebrated . . . abundance," love. She knows the odds are against her finding permanence and certainty in an unsafe world: "the tall / clock in the corner" is steadily ticking, but the persona has courage, wit, and faith (not necessarily religious) to see her through this journey. The clock's ticking is not just time running out; it is also "the beat of a faithful heart."

"The Hospitality of Chairs" reveals the persona's need to reclaim cast-off chairs "piled aloft in Floyd's / abandoned barn." She has to work hard at resurrecting the chairs, scouring with "chemical, steel wool, and grit / the chamfered stretchers, foliated rails, / bellflowers and acanthus carved by hand." Her effort is rewarded as beneath her palm "the first faint flush / of cherry hardwood rises." Then a turn occurs in the final stanza when she hopes her act of reclamation will bring about for her a kind of immortality when, her "name and face erased from memory," a family sits down in these hospitable chairs in "a radiant room at dusk."

"Kites," while focusing on lost kites, hints at the salvation offered by "groundless hope" and that "rare survivor one may find / Half hidden in the brittle winter weeds." The kite "rises— flutters," and, yes, "falls," but in this desperate attempt to reclaim flight, "some half-remembered dream of boundlessness" is celebrated.

The persona confesses in the next poem, "In November," that she has a "sneaking affection" for this month of "necessary death / Of burial and summing-up." And though the persona's mood only allows her to see Thanksgiving as a "sad, modest celebration," it is still a *celebration,* a time of family gatherings, of hospitality. This month also permits the persona to look at her life through Yeats's "cold eye," since the fields are "swept clean," and now there is "nothing of leaf / Or blossom to seduce / The eye." She can face more clearly "the hard / Unwavering line / Of the horizon."

"Unsafe Crossings" reveals a specific memory which the hard line of the horizon permits the persona to see. The scene depicts the traumatic death of the persona's childhood friend Jennie. It is an unsafe world, but as the adult persona recalls her friend's being hit by a car and somersaulted through the air, she can now sardonically "applaud the grace," the "daring" of her friend's death. Horror has been transformed into art. This transformation does not justify Jennie's death; it celebrates the act of dying, thereby (in this poem) reclaiming her friend.

"Unredeemed" celebrates another childhood friend Mary Margaret Duffy, but the poem mostly conveys the persona's

need for expiation, for her own redemption, for assuring
herself a place "among the tidy, / blameless dead" ("Consider
Socrates"): "I longed to whisper my transgressions, / feel
them dissipate and rise into the firmament / my mortal soul
scoured clean" ("Unredeemed").

"On Hearing of the Death of a Friend" emphasizes the
book's title, revealing the metaphor of "weakened heartwood
exposed, / falling away, the way it all falls / away." Loss
dominates this poem leading to the despair of the concluding
lines: "even love— / even that, in the end, falls away." And yet,
when the persona has completed her summing-up, her quest
for reclamation and expiation, she will be able to acknowledge
in the final poem of the book that "old love" is not consigned
to the grave ("Where Old Love Lies").

The next poem, "Will the Last One to Leave Please Turn
Out the Lights?," conveys the persona's stance for facing an
unsafe, loveless world: eat, drink, try to pretend she's merry,
and "show up /while the party's in full / swing." If, as she now
seems to believe, nothing lasts, then she might as well make the
best of it.

The problem, however, is that the persona can't stop
worrying, can't be merry, because she continues to chronicle
her "insufficiency— / another entry for the log / of failures I
keep close at hand" ("Pressure"). What she wants is not escape
from accountability, from her failings, but expiation. Her
nightmare reveals her "lost and unprepared / to take the test for
which I had no answers" ("Pressure"). This opening poem
sequence suggests that the persona's predominant concern is
with her own confrontation with death. *Will* she be able to face
that cup of hemlock blameless as Socrates?

"When the Second Chance Cloning Clinic Opens" offers
the possibility of avoiding death and loss by starting over and
this time being someone with an "audacious name—Carmen /
or Camille—something to live down or up to." If given a
second chance, the persona says she will bet her "sweet life on
luck," especially if everything falls away at the last. Her quest,
however, will reveal that everything of value *doesn't* fall away,
and luck can run out.

"Not Writing a Poem" provides another option for
escaping to "another place"; in this case the medium is
language, and when it, too, fails, the persona may cry out
like the old Roman grammarians calling on their gods, their
Genius.

"'Provide, Provide'" alludes to Robert Frost's poem by the
same title, but the speaker in Miriam Vermilya's poem is not as
bitter as Frost's. Miriam's persona can laugh at herself, at her
fate of "being one of the few / limp leaves still clinging to the
family / tree," of having survived most of her friends—"all
having / rushed ahead to the finish line." In planning her
funeral, she opts for "weeping, the rending of garments"; she
wants a big show, but she doesn't want her dentist, so she
winks at herself, even at death, and decides she'd best provide
some *new* friends.

"Summerfield's Steakhouse, Detroit" reveals the persona
on the lookout for these new friends. She finds them in a group
of Jewish women gathered for a reunion at the steakhouse,
"their grief a low hum beneath / the scrape of cutlery on china,
their bodies / taut, leaning farther into the circle." The poem's
persona would like to be invited into this circle, to become
more than an eavesdropper indulging in imagining herself a
member of this group, these "survivors," offering up her "own
litany / of loss." Her celebrating the survivors, these women,
anticipates upcoming sections, as does the persona's desire to be
part of a family, feel a hand against her cheek and hear one of
the women, like a mother, calling her "Darling."

The final poem of the section, "Ode to Schultz Motors,"
sings the "divine celestial light" of Schultz Motors' used-car
lot—"a sea / of polished chrome" that revives the weary
persona returning from a trip "back / East." This glow provides
the persona with a "surge / of joy" assuring her that she will be
able to arrive home. Her faith is confirmed "along a road where
wire- / strung pennants hum hosannas in the cold."

The first section has introduced the thematic motifs which
the following three sections will develop as the persona
intensifies her quest to reclaim her family as she seeks expiation
for what she perceives as failures, leading to the final section in

which the persona can both forgive and receive forgiveness,
knowing that even though death will claim the corporal
body, love does not fall away.

Section II details the persona's need to reclaim her mother
and her father, her sister, her brother, and other family
members from the persona's lost childhood. She celebrates her
family of dancers, musicians, artists, poets—the lost and
beautiful creators of beauty.

The first two poems in this section, "My Mother's Lips"
and "Nitro," reveal the persona's mother to have been a woman
who could wear Scarlet Rage lipstick ("My Mother's Lips") and
later an "amulet" of nitroglycerin tablets in a "silver / vial
nestled in the cleft / between her breasts" ("Nitro"). She is a
woman hell-bent for life, even after strokes reduce her to
"straining to steer the wayward word from brain to tongue,"
that word being the essence of the woman who will not settle
for her daughter's Passion Pink lipstick. She demands scarlet:
"*Bright,* she whispers . . . *Brighter!*" ("My Mother's Lips"). Her
daughter would reclaim her youthful, vibrant mother if she
could, but the persona is "helpless and subdued," while her
mother's heart, even after the final stroke has exploded her
brain, "beat[s] on for half a day"("Nitro").

"Theme & Variations" is an elegy for the poet's father,
depicting him as a passionate musician "playing Rossini" on a
clarinet. The father has lost himself in the process: "he leans /
like a blind man toward the music stand / and turns the
dog-eared page he knows by heart." Everyone in the house is
transported out of the mundane and into dreams by the father's
"round, yearning notes," the "rushing *glissandi,*" the *"molto
allegro,"* and the *"con brio"* of the "final cadenza." The family is
carried away: "eighth-notes, / like small birds, lift from the
score."

The persona also tries to call back her piano-playing sister
in "'Heart and Soul'" and "Leaving." "'Heart and Soul'" reveals
that the sisters' mother is an accomplished pianist "who could
play Rachmaninov by sight / and almost anything by ear," but
her daughters at fourteen and twelve are not interested in the
"purgatory / of *Schirmer's First Piano Book.*" They fear the

metronome "ticking off [their] girlhood hours," so they
pound out 'Heart and Soul' *fortissimo* and sing "with the
world's / old hunger." The persona, however, now knows
that "the heart's merely / a muscle, unreliable at best." She
needs her sister back, but she is dead, having departed one
autumn with the geese, driving "a wedge through the empty
sky" ("Leaving").

The persona's brother is also dead. "Performance Art"
reveals that her brother, as a child, was an artist at dying: "the
elegance of his sinking— / slow, the languorous slide to earth."
Her brother (and his sister) could always rely on his returning
to life, taking a bow: "He knows what all the children know: /
that he will rise and rise again." He does not, however, stand
up after "the fist inside / his chest clamped down"
("Heartwood").

The title poem reveals the brother's passion for and skill at
carving wood, a sensuous art getting to the heart of the wood,
giving all until the heart stops, and his living sister has only one
of her brother's bowls as a replacement—"a narrow amber
trapezoid / with a handle like a club," a bowl made from the
redbud tree: *"not an easy wood— / you don't carve it; it carves
you, / it tells you what it wants to be."* Like poetry. Like, the
persona has discovered, relationships.

The next three poems sing the loss of more distant family
members, also artists. "Patchwork" celebrates "Aunt Jane,"
"Mother's / distant cousin, once or twice removed" who would
show up end of summer with her "thimble flashing desperate
coded signals" as she pieced quilts whose "stitches held for sixty
years this thread- / bare patchwork relic" the persona has used
to warm her "modest bed" and "read biography in four-inch
squares / of muslin, calico and flowered chintz"—the persona's
heritage: "wings that beat against a wall / of glass."

"The Banjo Player" reclaims a favorite uncle, "the
practitioner of every useless / thing"—magician, dancer, singer
for children. And then he lost his wife and two sons, and now
his right hand searches the banjo "for some forgotten / chord,
the stricken notes dim sparks / ascending from a feeble fire."

Even the persona's daring, adolescent mentor, Cousin
Charlotte, who would "slide and slither" her hips, "smoke
the pack of Luckys filched from Levy's / store," drink
"home-made brew" from Mason jars, and "shed her shirt and
shoes / and skirt to dance, bare-breasted, on the road" ("My
Cousin Charlotte, Dancing") has been transformed by time
into an old body in a wheelchair. No matter how hard the
persona tries to reclaim her dancing cousin, she can't: "when I
try to bring it back, to rouse the rash / insouciance, she says, *I
don't remember. / She says, That wasn't me.*"

The last poem in this section, "Cecropia," re-emphasizes
the motif of loss—"When I think of loss I think / of
Lizzie"—and looks back to the first poem in the section and
the mother's rage for a life that is *"Bright . . . Brighter!"* ("My
Mother's Lips") as well as looking ahead to the subject of
Section III—"the way it is with women, passed / like the black
queen in a game of hearts / from one man's hands into the /
next: named, renamed, nameless" ("Cecropia"). At the end of
"Cecropia," Lizzie and the persona hear "a voice calling / us in
from the dark," and as they approach the screen door, they are
"stunned in our tracks" finding the large North American
silkworm moth cecropia "pinned on the back / door screen."
Like the persona's mother calling for *Brighter* lips, the moth as
well as young Lizzie and the persona are driven by the "lust for
light."

In Section III, the persona appears to have stopped for the
moment her summing-up, her quest for expiation, but what
she has done, in actuality, is to travel a wider, less personal path
toward dealing with her loss, her guilt, her rage. Just as she
seems about to move from having reclaimed her parents and
siblings to considering the meaning of her relationship with her
husband, she appears hesitant to confront these feelings, taking
instead a wider view of male-female, husband-wife
relationships. She seems to want to see her situation in relation
to the generalized history of how men treat women before she
can focus on her own situation. Section III allows the persona
to present other women's stories, which actually are only one
story: the loss of paradise—Eve resigned to living with a

husband who seems content to avoid sharing any blame (and guilt) for this loss and who may, as he chooses, be violent or indifferent toward his wife, and who has certainly forgotten the passion, the fun of those early days in the Garden. Even though the tone of this section is primarily dark and bitter, the persona often retains her sardonic sense of humor, especially in the first three poems of the section.

"Wa'hela Tells Her Side" allows Lot's wife to sum up her life prior to having become a pillar of salt. She, like the book's persona, is also concerned with the question of blame and whether or not she can receive expiation: "Was it so terrible—that I turned back / for one last look?" Her life was the life of wives: teaching her daughters to patch clothing and prepare meals, washing her husband's feet, filling the lamps with oil "against the night." She has resigned herself to her role of actions, not words: "What a woman does is what she is." Like the mother in "My Mother's Lips" calling for *"Bright . . . Brighter!"* lipstick and Lizzie and the persona lusting "for light" ("Cecropia"), Wa'hela declares, "I was the light." She says she looked back "to fill my eyes / with what I knew was lost, and true," and she also dared look back because God ("His voice") had deigned "to tell a woman where / to cast her eyes." The poem concludes with Wa'hela's question asked with a tone of defiance, awe, and guilt: "I ask, am I to blame? / Was it my fault?"

The persona's interpretation of Edouard Manet's painting *Le Déjeuner sur l'Herbe* is likely the most sardonically funny ever written. The question seems to be: What is wrong with this picture? More specifically, what is wrong with these two men "lounging / on the grass," comparing "recent root canals," citing "baseball stats"? Are they unaware of (or just indifferent to, maybe satiated with) the beautiful, naked woman (both wife and lover) sighing, "bemused" beside them? No wonder she is about to "set loose her hair to rage sienna / in the sun." Once again the persona echoes the motif of Scarlet Rage for women.

If romance is missing from this threesome having a picnic on the grass, then it is not even an option for the spider-veined women perched on padded stools at happy hour or congregated

"at four o'clock in fluorescent / cafeterias" ("Early Birds"). In
their hearts, "they're still / just girls, girls who know / the
score": they are behind, and it's the bottom of the ninth. The
fact that in "a prior venue," they were "more than likely
princesses" led "virginal, to the tactile revels / of the marriage
bed" means nothing now. There don't seem to be any men
around, or if there are, they must be just as satisfied with
themselves as the two men ignoring their picnic's naked point
of interest. Sadly, these happy-hour / cafeteria women's "gifts"
go "unnoticed and untaken" ("Early Birds").

The next poem, "The Same Old Story," contains no
humor. The rage in this scene is the "fury" of a psychopath
"cruis[ing] the land," looking for a local woman to murder and
stuff into a dumpster. For the persona, however, the most
painful realization is not that men take out their rage on
women, but that "Local woman missing!" is only a sentence,
not a headline, on "the front page / toward the bottom." And
when the woman's body is returned, "transformed" some
"rainy spring," "she will be / buried on page four." The persona
wonders if the woman realized how unimportant she was.

Woman / wife as victim is presented in a different fashion
in "Ten Items or Less." Young Eve is out of the Garden and in
the supermarket "caught / between the Red Delicious / and the
Yellow Grimes." In one palm, she "cups a perfect apple / as if
she means to gauge / the weight." The other hand "clutches" a
shopping cart where her child rides like a toddler cowboy, "his
mouth / contorting to shriek." The persona understands why
the young woman drops the apple—"too heavy, or perhaps / it
was not what she / wanted after all."

And yet, passion is probably what got the young wife in
this fix, and the persona knows the day will come when this
young mother will become one of "these women of a certain
age" ("Remembering the Horses"). She, too, will "lean, arms
crossed on morning tables, staring / into cups of coffee
growing cold," and she will either choose to think of "last beans
/ to be picked from summer's / wrecked gardens" or remember,
instead, those "horses limned in ink"—passionate symbols

"bursting notebooks / with their heaving flanks, / their
hooves striking sparks" ("Remembering the Horses").

The persona acknowledges that it is unlikely that long-married wives can readily recall a time when their husbands desired "communion / in the sacred marriage bed" ("The Rector's Wife") and "ravenous— / couldn't get their fill"—"the shy / glimpse in lamplight of a naked body" ("Part of the Bargain"). The stark reality for such a wife is finding herself framed by a "leaded window," staring "out / at the barren ginkgo," waiting for her husband, having "given up / all hope of ever being first with anyone" ("The Rector's Wife").

An even starker reality is depicted in "Part of the Bargain" where in spite of the "solemn reaffirmations" of the older couple's wedding vows—for better or for worse, in sickness and in health—a year hence, this long-faithful wife will find herself spooning "soup / into his mouth" and half dragging, half carrying him to the bathroom. This part of her bargain will continue "week after week until she can / no longer bear the weight." Is it any wonder then that the persona prefers to leave the couple reaffirming their wedding vows, eating "their cake in celebration— / in remembrance of a pure endurance" ("Part of the Bargain")?

"Washing the Clothes of the Dead" proclaims that it is the wives, the women, who are faithful to the end even when burdened with "the worst of miscreants." "At the end, there is always a woman / who keeps the faith," keeps up appearances.

In "Naming the Birds," Belle admits that she has remained faithful to Henry's wishes even after his death. She has kept the bird feeder filled and knows the names of each bird. Now, in the nursing home, Belle can find relief from her chore: "Here they got / no use for birds," but she can't forget their names, because their names show "who you are or what / you do": *"northern shrike, whip-poor-will, night-hawk, butcher bird."* These are the names that "fly round" inside her head, names seemingly more appropriate for this widow than *Belle*, names that suggest women's Scarlet Rage.

"Reclamation" is an appropriate poem to close this section and anticipate the final one. Having spoken through the voices of disgruntled, disillusioned wives and women, the persona has readied herself to speak in Section IV of her own grief in love, to forgive and receive forgiveness. She will face Yeats's horseman blameless, able to acknowledge that love does not have to fall away at the end. Before she can attain this state of grace, she has to restore her lost estate, to "claim [her] own lost paradise," so "Reclamation" reveals a metaphorical link between the "wily Sumac," the displaced Native Americans, and wives. It is not coincidental that Miriam Vermilya has the tomahawk-wielding braves "storm the fortress of the *kitchen* door" [italics mine]. Like Native Americans reclaiming their land from the Anglos, the wives are reclaiming themselves, restoring their worth and dignity by declaring to their husbands, to men: "This time beads and trinkets won't suffice."

Section IV concludes the persona's summing-up, singing the lost. She is staring Yeats's horseman in the eye. She is now ready to resolve her need for confession and expiation, for acceptance and love (or at least for what she will settle for as love). The persona's tone is no longer sardonic, but it isn't maudlin either. It is a tone of reconciliation, of acceptance, even of discovery: there *is* something left at the end, something that survives, something infinite.

Section IV seems the most personal of all the sections, maybe because the moment has almost come for the persona to take her place "among the tidy, / blameless dead" ("Consider Socrates"), maybe because in this final section, most of the poems seem to focus on a long-struggling relationship between a man and a woman, seemingly the persona and her husband; so as the first poem, "Another Season," sets the tone for this section, it also seems to plead for one more season of "thrash and thrust," of sleek, iridescently arrogant drakes, "their sex-besotted / hens behind." The poem also suggests that the persona does not want to be "one alone": "Unchosen / or abandoned." She recalls her friend who has died and "ardently" wishes for another season, for love.

"Interior Weather" seems more confessional than instructional. The persona could be referring only to herself, but it seems more likely that when she refers to *you* standing

"by the black window / yearning for the gold / of a rising
day," to *you* waiting for "the creak of the copper / rooster in
its slow hard turning," she is not only expressing her own
"sorrow, / the color of iron clamp[ing] / down like the jaws of a
vise," but also that of a second person who feels the "winds of
the past blow cold / over marked and unmarked graves." The
sequence of poems in this section suggests that this person is
the persona's husband. Like his wife, he also hears the "winds
of the past" "whisper ancient quarrels, / last words spoken
carelessly, / or carelessly unspoken." Both wife and husband
seem to understand that no expiation is available; all the couple
knows is "the brassy taste of unpayable, / unpaid debts." Both
yearn for their lost paradise. Both desire the cold winds of their
past griefs to move in a different direction.

As the next poem "False Spring" reveals, this turning, this
thawing, is not easy. The couple is used to gathering in their
spirits when they feel "the bite / Of sleet, the sting of ice, the
snowy whirl—" of a wintry relationship. They are used to
holding tight to their emotions, withdrawing into themselves as
"a modest girl will gather in her skirts." What they are not
ready for is the "fluke" of Spring's arriving "full-blown in
March," the tyrannic sun's demanding "frozen sap to rise,"
revealing that the couple wants to experience "the early thaw."
They desire to give up their prideful "perseverance" and cease
to hold fast in winter. The irony, of course, is that when the
couple give in to passion, they realize this new season is "a
fluke." It is a false spring. Winter's "icy vise" clamps down
again, but hope for this relationship is implied in the
inevitability that the true spring will eventually arrive.

The couple must endure until the real thaw comes, but as
"To Build a Fire" reveals, their wintry relationship will not
catch fire, the "stubborn, soft green / heartwood sulks,
untempered in the stove." Tempers flare, and the couple
reaches "for shawls, another sweater," not for each other. They
smolder alone, seemingly lacking "the stuff from which good
fires / are made."

And yet, "Windows" develops the conceit of the couple
(who seem husband and wife) desiring to communicate, to

touch as they come together to wash window panes that shiver at the pressure of hands (the couple on separate sides of the fragile glass) beginning to "circle, counter-circle, . . . / meet and part." They have been together a long time, having washed windows "so many / years together we could do it / with our eyes shut tight." This time, however, the persona considers, as "the old pane shivers," how easily she could lose her husband. His hand (maybe as the result of "some sudden / rage") could shatter the glass that separates the couple, resulting in his arm being cut on the "vicious shards." The wife has been in this relationship too long to panic at the thought. She seems more surprised at what could (even now or *especially* now) be the consequence of this long, precarious relationship.

"North from Dahlonega" brings the persona to the turning point in her relationship with her husband, and this is also the turning point in her looking back at her life. Her summing-up has led her to this remembered scene, this moment when the couple's *unloving* built to a climactic turning. After twelve "miles of silence" in the car returning the couple *home,* ironically, to "the walls of separate rooms"—their compartmentalized emotions, they find themselves facing a choice. The road forks, and they can take "the long / safe way around" or "choose the crow's way, up and over" this mountain. In turning toward the shorter, more precarious road home, the couple are forced to work together to negotiate the dense cloud—the persona hanging out "the window to recite aloud / the yellow hieroglyphics of the road," while her husband, "hands on the wheel," follows her voice "around the hairpins to the peak." The mountain is "holding its breath, holding us." For a moment, the persona seems to want "to say / the wrong word," slide them "over the brink" and into "the onrushing void," but she doesn't. The couple communicate, and what the persona remembers for sure is their "coasting down the last mile, [her husband's] thumb raised in the victory sign," his face turned toward his wife. He was smiling "as we broke into the sunlight where the town / spread itself, roof and chimney, like a banquet." There is no doubt that a breakthrough has occurred, an epiphany begun.

"The Nearsighted" confirms that love requires a close-up
study, not the wide-angled shot. The persona now recognizes
that touch—the microscopic, "myopic," "minuscule"
approach—is the only way to see "life pulsing," to "gauge a
planet's girth," or know love. Lovers cannot know each other
from "across the street"; they require a closer view, knowing
"by heart an arm's curve, the amber chip / in one gray eye, the
way a slow smile blooms," reminiscent of the smile of the
persona's husband as they coasted down the mountain and
"broke into the sunlight" ("North from Dahlonega").

The final three poems of the book confirm the persona's
epiphany that it is not true what she thought early in her
summing-up, not true that "love . . . / even that, in the end,
falls away" ("On Hearing of the Death of a Friend"). "Love,"
the first of the last three poems, admits that theirs is not the
romance of Prince Charming and the Princess riding off on a
white charger to live happily ever after. This is love at the end
of a long marriage. The persona no longer needs to ask if her
husband loves her, not because she knows the answer to the
question, but because "the answer wouldn't matter. / You
wanted me, I wanted you. / We are married." And "that / is
that," a fact confirmed by *acts* of love: the persona's rubbing
her husband's hands "to take away the ache," the husband
"sometimes late / at night . . . fumbling / with the blanket,
covering [his wife's] shoulders, keeping [her] from the cold."

"Ephemeroptera" does not deny that our lives and
institutions are indeed ephemeral: "the Ebenezer Baptist
church, / its door agape, declines daily / into dust and rubble."
The church graveyard's tombstones are "listing / or broken or
gone." A few markers bear "words now scarcely visible: / Eliza,
Beloved Wife . . . In Perpetual. . . . " In a million years, "the
stricken / stones will be scoured clean," but love—the "tumult /
of mating"—will continue to "rise each spring" with every
hatch of mayflies, "consummate, immortal." Ephemerids
"dance above the clouded waters."

At the end of her quest, her life-view, the persona can
declare that Old Love surely does not lie in the grave ("Where
Old Love Lies"). Yes, "bone and flesh" decompose—the

corporal "cargo of death," but "love must engender a critical
mass, / its energy transformable—directional." She knows
this must be the case, because she has "known the singular
kiss / that burns the lips for decades after." She is no longer
worried about expiating her life's transgressions, about needing
her "mortal soul scoured clean" ("Unredeemed") before taking
her place "among the tidy, / blameless dead" ("Consider
Socrates"). What she has found at the end is better than a clean
slate, better than reclaiming all her lost family and friends, even
better than surviving. The beating, faithful heart she knows,
now, is *love,* a love that transcends *(survives* if you will) "the
decomposing particles" lovers leave behind. Love, hard-won
and often grief-stricken, contains a "half-life" that "lingers in a
stone, a bench, / the pavements" where family, friends, lovers,
husbands and wives walked. Love does not fall away. It lingers,
drifts, glimmers, rising from the ashes of the dead, alive in the
"infinite air."

Robert Fink
Abilene, Texas, 1999

HEARTWOOD

recumbent
on his cot, draped in a freshly
laundered toga, beard shampooed
and fluffed, the cup of hemlock
in his hand—how certainly,
the night before, he'd sorted
through his aphorisms, taking
care to jettison any less-than-
cogent thoughts.
                    We all say
we want it to be sudden: a light-
ning bolt to the brain, a stutter
in the arteries, then sleep, or
something like it—our hands still
clutching the rake or an atlas
turned to a map of Afghanistan,
but wouldn't it be better to know?
A three-month
                    warning
would be nice; you'd want to burn
those letters nestled in a shoebox
on the closet shelf, finish up
the pint of Seagram's hidden
in the desk's third drawer and
trash the butt-sprung underwear
a derelict would be ashamed
to wear
            to any accident,
the way, before embarking on a trip
to Buffalo or Budapest, one feels
compelled to mend the toaster,
broken since last New Year's day

and polish up the silver candle-
sticks turned umber on the cupboard
shelf. Some sort
                    of portent
would be helpful (nothing morbid
or alarming) an angel, or your mother,
say, appearing in a dream to whisper
August second, or *September tenth,*
just time enough to put your house
in perfect order before you take
your place among the tidy,
blameless dead.

I

The earliest one in my memory
was tall, white, and austere—
and at the curb a black, high-
shouldered hearse waiting;
a house where death,
pausing at the front parlor
was livelihood, where once
my grandfather—having
gathered up a body
from the railroad track—
put it, like a jigsaw
puzzle, back together.

II

One August in Albany, Indiana
the house behind the railroad
tracks went up in flames,
the whole town gathered,
their faces lit and tilted
upward as if awaiting
the epiphany that would change
everything, and the sound
of a child's thin voice calling
Lucky . . . Lucky . . . Come!

III

Newly wed, I lived for a time
with scorpions and snakes
in a tarpaper hovel
whose walls were daily
assailed by swirling wind-

blown dust—a shotgun shack—
each room leading, straight
as a Texas highway, to the back
and the bed where nightly
we celebrated our abundance.

IV

The abandoned ones—
shipwrecked in a sea
of chicory and Queen Anne's
lace—can lure me down
a rutted lane to breach
the unlatched kitchen
door and listen
to the vagrant voices
whispering of the day
the binder took poor
Harvey's arm, of taxes
due, and cows gone dry.

V

Driving down a city street
or country lane, don't you
sometimes harbor a secret
wish to be inside the houses
flowing by, to witness
lives surely more dramatic
than your own, or to wander
undetected through the hallways
testing mattresses, opening
the cupboards, trying
on their clothes—
trying on their skins?

VI

And what do we leave behind
in the houses we've lived in
and left—a hand-made valentine,
perhaps, stuck in the baseboard
behind the stove, a paraplegic
doll slumped in a dark corner
of the basement, and almost
always a dog, asleep
beneath the hillside grass.

VII

Far from home—in Nassau
or West Palm Beach—I think
of our house beneath
a lacy shawl of snow, eyes
shuttered, the furnace
sighing in the basement,
refrigerator humming
itself to sleep, the tall
clock in the corner—
its steady ticking
the beat of a faithful heart.

It's clear these chairs have taken more
than one shellacking—piled aloft in Floyd's
abandoned barn, back to rail, seat to stile,
their spires and angles
                                formed for years
a cityscape for sparrow, pigeons, mice,
their once-sleek skin of varnish blighted
to black runnels by the rain and sun
that breached the ruined roof.

One deeply dented seat, its mohair cover
worn to shine, suggests (from some departed
life) a broad and pompous bottom, dark
waistcoat, steely eyeglass rims, their warnings
flashing in the falling light
                                while another,
scarcely dimpled, speaks of a gentler
presence: a slender torso held erect by corsets
boned and stiff with stays, the sibilant
sweep of bombazine against a polished table
leg; the evening light crepuscular, dark
corners and the scent of kerosene.

I scourge with chemical, steel wool, and grit
the chamfered stretchers, foliated rails,
bellflowers and acanthus carved by hand.
Now, beneath my palm, the first faint flush
of cherry hardwood rises
                                and I think upon a distant
day—my name and face erased from memory,
unfamiliar voices raised in argument or song,
a radiant room at dusk, white damask
and the table set.

Whatever happens to the kites we fly
In March, that rise and soar like groundless hope
Cartwheeling in the matrix of the sky
Bright chips inside a child's kaleidoscope.
Forgotten on a dusty shelf, a few
May linger—torn, de-tailed and broken-spined,
But most just vanish, as the seasons do . . .
Except that rare survivor one may find
Half hidden in the brittle winter weeds,
Pale ghost of spring's exuberant excess.
It rises—flutters—falls, as if it heeds
Some half-remembered dream of boundlessness,
Caught between the stern reality
Of pragmatic fence and unrelenting tree.

I confess a sneaking affection
For the eleventh month
The bittersweet gone
Back to its roots, sunk
Deep into an earthy Zen
And we return to our caves
If a room lit by fire
Can be called a cave
A time of necessary death
Of burial and summing-up
The month that promises
Nothing—offering only
One sad, modest celebration
The fields swept clean
And nothing of leaf
Or blossom to seduce
The eye, allowing us to see
More clearly the hard
Unwavering line
Of the horizon.

We walked as we always did
to the corner, heads together,
lips sweet with schoolyard
secrets; she paused at the curb
as she had been taught, leaned
out to look, then ran across
to the concrete island.
When she turned to wave,
her mouth stretched to a gap-toothed
grin and one of us called out:
See you tomorrow!

Then her body was in the air
and I thought of somersaults,
clumsy cartwheels, and the two
of us collapsed, giggling
on the grass, but this . . .
this was perfection: her spine
arched to a taut, clean line,
toes together and pointed
down in a flawless flip;
and her skull where it met
the pavement made a single
sound like the sound of a pair
of hands clapping once
to applaud the grace of her daring.

Turned as she was to wave good-
bye, she couldn't have seen it
coming—but surely, she must have
sensed a perturbation of air,

must have felt the ground shudder
beneath her feet as the Buick,
bucking, mounted the curb.

The driver was not cited, being
dead before the impact and Jennie,
being dead, was not indicted for
presuming safety there, or anywhere.

Unredeemed

Saturdays—the time of day when shadows of the tree-
   lawn elms would drape themselves like scarves
across the summer sidewalks—we'd drop our jacks
   and jump ropes, watch as Mary Margaret Duffy
drifted by, fresh from her confession, her socks
   immaculate below unblemished knees, a wisp
of linen, like a benediction, floating on her head.

   What wouldn't I have given for her small
superior smile, the beads she carried in her purse,
   access to the carved and mullioned doors
of Our Lady of the Rosary, the air inside dense
   with tears and blood, her Christ a paint and plaster
movie star large as life above the altar while
   in the basement of the Redkey Baptist Church

our Jesus, bland and mild, gazed meekly
   from a Kresge nine-by-twelve hung above
our heads. I coveted her iniquities—the muttered
   sins passed through a grill, the listening ear,
the bended knee, the expiating murmured prayers;
   I longed to whisper my transgressions,
feel them dissipate and rise into the firmament
   my mortal soul scoured clean.

The very air of the room where you are
sitting or just standing by the window
rarifies, retracts, reminds how everything
falls away—family, friends, whatever
can be known and loved falls away.
Beyond the window, stillness—

the morning world bowed down
in silence, life lines sagging ground-
wise, bush, branch and vine strangled
by the ice born of a late winter storm.
Shuddering, the sycamore bends
beneath its burden, brought to its
knees with a sound like gunshot,

weakened heartwood exposed,
falling away, the way it all falls
away: branch and twig, friend
and brother, even madness, stilled
at last, even sorrow, even love—
even that, in the end, falls away.

Will the Last One to Leave Please Turn Out the Lights?

Come late rather than early—
better not be first to arrive
to pace alone in the bright
scrubbed light while
in the kitchen the hostess
is busy discovering fire;
better to show up
while the party's in full
swing, after the wheel's
been invented, when
others of your kind
are gathered, dancing
cheek to cheek,
taking care to leave
well before the fights
break out, before
your eyes begin to water
from the smoke, the last
ice cube melting
in the sink and all
the soldiers dead, to slip
away before the window
bars slide closed,
the host nowhere to be
found, and the door
swings shut
with a sinister click.

As the column of mercury rises and the black
   band tightens around my arm, it seems
      we both are in mourning,

the way she sighs and turns away to record
   the chronicle of my insufficiency—
      another entry for the log

of failures I keep close at hand—her face
   above the white coat as sorrowful
      as Mrs. Margrove's

the day I was the ruination of her Student
   Spring Recital, when my hands froze
      on the ivory keys

the black notes of the score indecipherable
   as Sanskrit, my heart plunging
      downward with

the upsurge of blood threading its way
   against gravity to flame
      my cheeks,

cheeks that burned each time Miss Vogel
   stood before my sixth-grade
      desk, the blue-lined

paper, emblazoned with its scarlet letter
   D, held in her hand, her face
      an amalgam

of pity and displeasure—a scenario repeated
as recently as Thursday night
in the nebulous

corridors of sleep where, wearing a flimsy
paper husk, I found myself
lost and unprepared

to take the test for which I had no answers,
a turbulence of blood drumming
in my veins.

I want to be first in line, shivering on the sidewalk
in my thin investment of acceptable genes
like a star-struck groupie waiting for the Doors
to open on a new-born world of strobing lights.
Imagine holding in your arms the one you love

most, double helix doubled, identical alleles
aligned in perfect synchrony, blueprint for
a transcendental life, the whole thing calling
first for some audacious name—Carmen
or Camille—something to live down or up to.

As to advice, wear red shoes and midnight-
blue mascara; dance the tango with dark,
mysterious men; fall in love less often,
or oftener but not so hard; squander your
inheritance and bet your sweet life on luck.

Today my head wants to go to another place,
take leave—so to speak—of my senses
away from the uncomely constructs of my mother

tongue, perhaps to Rome, but in the age
of Cicero declaiming on the Forum steps
in syntax best described as high-falutin'.

How elevated—how dignified the language—
how much less reprehensible, to be caught
in flagrante delicto, instead of *in the sack*

with Darlene K., such lapses to be alibied
away by placing blame on some mischief-
making god or goddess—I'd bet on Venus

of the dozen deities who power the wheels
of daily commerce: Janus, for opening
the year, Terminus, to close the gates.

You know the rest . . . excluding certain
household gods who hang around the kitchen
tasting soup or dozing on a corner bench

and those *ad hominem* demigods, available
for consultation night or day. Picture,
if you will, the old grammarians who pace

the Tiber's banks invoking those sweet spirits,
how—when words fail and eloquence eludes—
they cry aloud, *O Juno! O my Genius! Awake!*

On my way to the dentist I plan
my funeral—it being that kind of day—
the sky an El Greco gray, with an argosy
of umber clouds riding its choppy

surface, and my jaw throbbing
accompaniment to something suitably
doleful playing on the radio.
When my friend, Margretta, understood

her three-year bout with cancer was not
to be a draw, she said unequivocally
No sad songs. How I wish she could
have seen the faces of the mourners

when they stepped inside the chapel
to the funky syncopations of "Fig Leaf Rag."
But that's not me. I want the tearful
voice of the pipe organ, "Abide With Me";

I want weeping, the rending of garments,
gladioli and iris in wretched excess
and a full house—the last, I admit,
unlikely, my being one of the few

limp leaves still clinging to the family
tree; and the roll call of friends
I might have counted on: George,
Glendine, Eldon and Jo and the others,

unavailable now as guests, all having
rushed ahead to the finish line. I consider
inviting my dentist, who breathes
spearmint and solicitude, soon to be

bending above my body laid out
on the brown Naugahyde, but think
better of it, and send myself a mental
note: *Find new friends. Provide.*

Their faces, ransomed to adversity and time
yet appealing still—Leah, of the amazing
henna hair, diamond-studded Judy; Sarah,

swathed in folds of cobalt blue; Sylvia
and Rebecca, who could have been Zoe Friedman's
mother—the same assertive nose, the same

sinuate wreath of hair, coarse as sisal, her bosom
soft enough and broad enough, your head could
make of its hillocks a feather pillow—

whose kitchen—redolent of chicken fat, pastrami,
and patchouli—I haunted all one year, hungry
for the feast of her prodigious kindness.

She must have thought it strange that her girl-chick—
her own precocious Zooey—would favor
for a season this pale Protestant,
this goyish child . . . .

A reunion, I surmised,
of sorts: Leah from Biloxi, Sylvia, all the way
from Little Rock, their faces luminous

with laughter, then solemn as they turned
from *Remember when* . . . to till the fertile fields
of sorrow, the green ones and the ones well-

plowed, names of men and places: Jacob . . .
Moise . . . Krakow . . . their grief a low hum beneath
the scrape of cutlery on china, their bodies

taut, leaning farther into the circle, Auschwitz
in their eyes. But that's just speculation, pure.
The truth is, they may just as well have been

speaking of a handyman . . . a cousin . . . a favorite
kosher butcher . . . . And isn't that the way it always
is with eavesdroppers—the story never straight

the muddle of the middle, beginnings blurred
by wishful alterations, endings only guessed at,
the way I guessed at theirs: every year

diminishment, the circle growing smaller,
like the loop of a noose at each pull of the rope
until . . . but again, conjecture, a chronic habit

I indulge in, as I did that day, the waitress
hovering, pencil poised, asking what I wanted.
What I wanted was to tap my spoon against

the coffee cup, stand up and raise my glass,
Shalom, to all survivors. No. What I wanted
was to drag my chair across the aisle into

their empty space and offer up my own litany
of loss. No, what I really wanted was to walk
into Rebecca's arms, feel her hand against my cheek
and hear her call me *Darling . . . Bubeleh.*

That divine celestial light—so often seen
by those whose lives are teetering on the brink
and the soul escapes like steam to hover over
the cold and torpid body—makes me think,
sometimes, of a certain used-car lot set down
between a field of clover and a field of corn
along Route Nine three miles from town,

how, coming home from trips we'd take back
East, ten hours of asphalt gone, and more to go
on narrow country roads where overhead
the trees form frigid tunnels down below
and faltering spirits sink, and I, near dead,
massage my stiffening fingers on the wheel
(the heater having quit twelve miles ago).

Then, faintly from the North there comes
a glow that bounces from a sea
of polished chrome, and I feel the surge
of joy those others know, as freezing
travelers feel a warm room and a fire eight
miles from home along a road where wire-
strung pennants hum hosannas in the cold.

11

Weekday afternoons I'd watch her
at the mirror, working the stick's
exacting glide upward to the apex

downward to the cleft, the sure pass
across the lower curve, her lips rolled
inward, tightly pressed, as if to seal them

against some secret thought's escape.
And once, the tube open in her hand,
she held my face to coat my mouth

with Scarlet Rage, then lifted me
above the mirror's rim to see our twin
manufactured smiles. And something

then—a riddle or a question—passed
behind her eyes, enough to make her
snatch her hanky from the pocket

of her dress, and swipe it, hard,
across my mouth . . . . Now, turned sideways
in her chair, she stares at me, my casual

sweep of Passion Pink, her hand
trembling, lifting across her breast,
her index finger pointing to a corner

of her mouth. I place my hand
beneath her chin, stroke the pale cosmetic
grease. In the mirror her mouth contorts,

unsatisfied. *Blight*, she breathes, and shakes her head. *Bride*, she says, straining to steer the wayward word from brain to tongue.

Bright, she whispers . . . *Brighter!*

On days when the wind pauses,
poised to turn, the detonations generate
a sympathetic trembling in the blood.
I watched them once from the road,
men and machines blasting stone
from the ruined belly of the earth;
in the fields nearby, the ironweed
and goldenrod, stiff with gray dust,
the sycamore tipped upside down,
its thick, arterial roots stretched
skyward, sucking the dry air.

My mother wore it on a chain
around her neck, an amulet
against abuse, a glance, a word,
a slight, real or imagined—
anything—would send her
fingers fumbling for the silver
vial nestled in the cleft
between her breasts while we,
helpless and subdued,
watched the ritual played out:
a single tablet underneath
the tongue, the shudder
of relief at the percussive
ebbing in her chest, the faint,
forgiving smile.

In the end, it didn't matter.
Unaccountable, that final stroke—
the flash inside her brain a clean
explosion. Her stubborn heart,
I'm told, beat on for half a day.

For D. E. Manring
1904-1963

In a room at the back of the house my father
is playing Rossini, his jacket looped over
the back of a chair, his clarinet lifted
tenderly, from its slender sarcophagus.

Upstairs in a bedroom someone is writing a letter.
The round, yearning notes of the intro infuse her
with longing; she sighs, drops her pen,
looks down at her hands, she thinks
about hands, the hands embracing the ebony
horn; she thinks of the hands of her lover:
fingertips blunt, the pale, fine hairs . . . .

My father sways, his eyelids drooping, he leans
like a blind man toward the music stand
and turns the dog-eared page he knows by heart.

On the porch in a chair someone is reading a book
or pretends to; the rushing *glissandi,* climbing
then falling, sound like a car, the gears
of a car, the music they make revving up, shifting
down; he imagines himself in a Crosley convertible,
wind combing his hair; he imagines a red and white
pump, a full tank of gas, cheap and unrationed.

My father's head nods *molto allegro* as if
in agreement, the toe of his shoe hits the hardwood
in a steady, percussive, eight/quarter beat.

In the kitchen, someone is stirring a pot of soup
made of scraggly beef and tomatoes picked
from her Victory garden; the cascading passage
that pours from his horn reminds her of water,
a fountain in Paris, and behind the hotel,
the gardens and greensward where once—
at midnight—they lay on the grass . . . .

My father is playing Rossini. He steals a half-
measure of breath as he scales, *con brio,*
the cliffs of the final cadenza, and the eighth-notes,
like small birds, lift from the score.

Fourteen and twelve, we were the despair
of Mrs. Margrove and our mother—

who could play Rachmaninov by sight
and almost anything by ear, who

each Saturday, would send us on flagging
feet down Euclid Avenue, a dollar

folded in our pockets to the purgatory
of *Schirmer's First Piano Book,*

a metronome encased in rosewood
ticking off our girlhood hours,

where, in turn, we laid waste
to "The Happy Farmer," stumbled

over "Für Elise" until, at last released,
we headed home to the one true

song, again and again, *fortissimo*—
my left hand, her right—the tremolo

of our voices filled with the world's
old hunger, dying, as we were,

to give our hearts and bodies
our inchoate souls. Who could have

told us then how the heart's merely
a muscle, unreliable at best, or

how much I would miss the press
of her knee against my own, her heart

and soul . . . her good right hand.

Always—this time of year—the sumac
blazes, its candles the blood color
that rushes to the cheek in a fever
of anticipation and the geese, who
in August floated the pond, asleep
below the dusty leaves of the willow,
now genuflect, wings fanning the air.
The spirit lifts at the prospect
of departure: in the pocket the coins'
impatient jingle, the glance toward
the darkened tunnel where, at the end,
the humming plane waits on the tarmac.
On the day of my sister's death,
I held her hand and whispered her name
but she had already turned her face
to the window to watch the geese
drive a wedge through the empty sky.

For Michael Manring
1927-1991

My brother was the boy most often marked
for death, so singular his skill at it.
I see him ambushed, back against a wall,
a chicken feather stiff above the rag
he'd tied around his head.
It is August—the immortal month—
the bleakness of the days
to come beyond imagining.

He stands there on a ridge of dirt, cornered,
and he knows it, his lips tight in a sardonic
smile, at his moment of undoing. The eyes
of his pursuers narrow, a finger aims
above a well-cocked thumb; one bullet
finds his naked chest, then a second
and another, his riddled body still
erect, fingers pressed against his heart;
slow, the hinge behind his knee unlocks—
slow, the elegance of his sinking—
slow, the languorous slide to earth—
one hand outstretched, a gasp of final
exhalation, no muscle's telling twitch
as seconds . . . minutes . . . pass.

But now, his crumpled legs unfold;
he springs up, pivoting, in so deep
a bow his feather sweeps the ground.
He knows what all the children know:
that he will rise and rise again.
Yet who would not admire the eloquence
of his passing—his gallantry in defeat?

My brother was a fool
for wood—grain and burl—
the heart of it; he never could resist
the lure of any well-turned finial
or baluster, would fondle the seductive
curves as if it were a woman's body.

That last time, he led
me to his shop to show the wooden
bowls he'd carved that lined
the shelf like trophies saying
Pick the one you like.
I chose the one I thought would suit

my bent—not the robust
rounded poplar, or the crenulated
oval teak, but a narrow amber trapezoid
with a handle like a club. *That one
is from the redbud tree,* he said,

*not an easy wood—
you don't carve it; it carves you,
it tells you what it wants to be.*
Unfit for fruit or dinner rolls, it has
its place here on the window sill
to hold the bills I mean to pay,
expired coupons, used ticket stubs.

I like to think
he'd just completed one of cherry wood
chipped and sanded, oiled and rubbed

to dazzlement when the fist inside
his chest clamped down, his heart's
blood slowing, the way a stream

          of water in a pipe will
falter when the clattering pump shuts
down—the way it could be some after-
noon when you've pressed the final
crimp around the crust of an apple
pie—fluted, sealed and signed.

Aunt Jane was what we called her, though
she wasn't aunt to anyone, but Mother's
distant cousin, once or twice removed.
She came each year around the time
when sunflower heads droop low and corn
stalks rustle with the smallest breeze
to wash the supper dishes, feed
the laying hens and piece the quilts
we sank beneath on autumn nights.

Day's end, she sorted discards saved all
year: the worn out, outgrown, out-of-style,
tugging on the cloth to uproot least-worn
parts—shirttails, hems of aprons, edges
ripped from cotton sheets transparent
in the center—then cut and stitched
the patches, edge to edge, her needle
stabbing with such ferocity as if
to dare the thing to come apart.

Those end-of-summer evenings we bruised
the side yard grass, bare heels as thick
as rawhide, split the air with heathen cries
and raced across the lawn to capture
lightning bugs in Mason jars, beneath
the window where she sat, head bent,
her thimble flashing desperate coded signals
in the yellow lamplight while all around
the locusts shrilled their urgent mating songs.

Before the first real snow we sent her on
to Cousin Belle's in Delaware, and turned
toward home, our Christian duty done 'til summer

came again. There must have come a time
we didn't need to meet the southbound train
or clear the bedroom in the back; I'm told
she died the spring of nineteen thirty-eight
or -nine in Maine, just halfway through
her block of time with Mother's Aunt Louise.

Her stitches held for sixty years this thread-
bare patchwork relic—not the sort of thing
you'd want to decorate a wall
but adequate to warm my modest bed.
I read biography in four-inch squares
of muslin, calico and flowered chintz:
the crush of August grass beneath a heel;
wings that beat against a wall
of glass; the cry of wheels across a rail-
bed switch; the locusts' song.

                                        Of the tribe
of uncles peopling the periphery of my child-
hood, he was the practitioner of every useless
thing—he could pluck a quarter from behind
an ear; execute a decent time step, shuffle, buck
and wing, sing passably on key.

                                        In the snapshot
he is all good-will and teeth—ebullience
in shades of black and gray—his body
straining forward like a man about to leap
the net to claim his handshake and the silver
cup, his left hand curled around the neck
of a five-string Mastertone.

                                        Summer evenings
we would commandeer the side-porch swing,
his fingers scrambling above the banjo's fret:
"Floatin' Down the River" or "Alabama
Jubilee," his buoyant tenor and my tenuous
soprano counter-point against the crickets
rasping in the grass.

                                        The year his wife
decamped, his enduring smile diminished
to a minor mode—the smile of one who
only half-believes the check is in the mail—

still, he had his sons to teach the harmonies
he knew and when they, grown up in love
with flight, propelled a Cessna straight
into a Georgia mountainside,

he wept and said,
At the end, at least, they had each other.
Tomorrow, or the next day, or the next,
he will lift his banjo from its felt-lined case,
his right hand searching for some forgotten
chord, the stricken notes dim sparks
ascending from a feeble fire.

It must have been the way
she walked, the slide and slither
of her hips beneath the crepe-de-chine
that made the mothers pull their daughters close
and caused new brides to clutch
their husbands' sleeves.

Point-man for the steamy swamps
of adolescence, Charlotte taught me how
to smoke the pack of Luckys filched from Levy's
store, took me to the house on Horse Shoe
Ridge where home-made brew filled
Mason jars, held my head the next day.

One night we took her father's
Nash, gears snarling like a junkyard
dog; she rammed it up the switch-back, hair-
pin turns to where Old Baldie flattens out before
the final tree-line fringe, while down
below the dark town slept.

Spotlighted in the yellow beams
Charlotte shed her shirt and shoes
and skirt to dance, bare-breasted, on the road,
"Bolero" throbbing like a heartache from the radio.
I knew then I wanted to be Charlotte
and knew I never could.

I see her once or twice a year,
I push her chair along the brickwork
path; we speak of weather—family—food,
but when I try to bring it back, to rouse the rash
insouciance, she says, *I don't remember.*
She says, *That wasn't me.*

In the Hall of Entomology I pause
before a glass-topped case, remembering
how we loved to say the names: Polyphemus

Cecropia, Pandora Sphinx,
How many years . . . driven, farther, deeper
into the vanishing forest—anonymous, alive.

When I think of loss I think
of Lizzie, granny glasses halfway down
her nose, her pale, perspiring face intense,

of creeping through the Limberlost
of Krueger's third-growth woods, nets
we made from loops of wire and cast-off

front-room curtains, the summer
when we took an oath in mingled blood
to eschew the frivolous, to have no truck

with boys, to be scholarly and
profound. All that before the serious
blood, the breasts that bloomed in spite

of everything, the boys who
metamorphosed into demigods,
whose names we coveted, wild to shed

our paternal labelings. Between us
we collected seven names—two fathers,
one step-father, four husbands (one lost

to death, one to incompatibility)—
the way it is with women, passed
like the black queen in a game of hearts

from one man's hands into the
next: named, renamed, nameless.
Little came of it, our brief excursion

into research: two tussocks,
three hawks and one specimen
preserved inside the jumbled schoolhouse

of my mind: a voice calling
us in from the dark. Lizzie and I
returned from the hunt across the grass

to the back porch steps—
stopped—stunned in our tracks,
sacrilege to move or speak,

unthinkable to raise
a net against the banded thorax
feathered palps and quivering wings

pinned on the back
door screen by lust for light.

Wa'hela, Lot's Wife
The Reader's Handbook

Was it so terrible—that I turned back
for one last look? It wasn't much, rough
cedar planks, one room for all of us, but
there I taught my daughters how to patch
our robes with linen thread and rub the new-
killed lamb with herbs; there I washed
my husband's feet with water from the village
well, filled the lamps with oil against the night.
What a woman does is what she is;
I was the light.

The screams, the cries for help were not
what made me look, not the flames and smoke
that rose; it was a door post painted blue
that made me stop and turn to fill my eyes
with what I knew was lost, and true, I heard
His voice demand obedience, yet I took it
with a grain of salt. It was absurd, I thought,
that he would deign to tell a woman where
to cast her eyes—I ask, am I to blame?
Was it my fault?

She tosses off her hat and cloak, kicks shoes aside
and turns to face the gentlemen lounging
on the grass,

her name, Giselle (perhaps Claudine); her lover
is the one who wears a ribboned hat, the other
one her husband.

In the middle-ground a white-clad figure stoops
(a compositional device to mark the apex
of the triangle).

The gentlemen lean forward, city faces solemn, compare
their recent root canals, their pale hands plucking
blades of grass.

She shimmies from her long black skirt, drops her muslin
crinolines, kicks off her cotton lace-trimmed
pantaloons.

The gentlemen are speaking now, in somber tones, of penny
stocks, debentures, bonds, gross national
product, golf.

Her bodice drops on the picnic basket; blushing peaches
spill; dark cherries roll like crimson marbles
on the ground.

Her lover gestures, finger raised, to make his point
concerning current baseball stats; her husband
concurs, nodding.

She sinks, half-smiling, down beside her spouse, sighs
and stares, bemused, at distant black-green trees.
In a moment

she will lift her arms, pull one by one the amber
pins, set loose her hair to rage sienna
in the sun.

Never mind the spider veins
embroidering their cheeks;
in their hearts they're still
just girls, girls who know
the score, at ease in their soft
bodies underneath the layered
linen, silk, Egyptian cotton.

In a prior venue they were
more than likely princesses,
each of them some doting
father's darling, coddled
and caressed, destined
to slip from paternal arms
into the seats of third-hand

Fords or Chevrolets, where
trembling hands would brush
across an anointed mound
of breast or thigh until one
suitor or another led them,
virginal, to the tactile revels
of the marriage bed.

Before my mother died she
said, *No one ever touches me.*
Not true. There were
the nurses and her children,
dutiful if nothing else—

but you know what she meant,
which may be why
the corners of their mouths

have given in to gravity,
and why—ubiquitous—
they perch on padded stools
at happy hour or congregate
at four o'clock in fluorescent
cafeterias, irascible
as starlings, their gifts
unnoticed and untaken.

Local woman missing!
Last seen jogging?
driving?
drinking in a bar
near Fourth and Clancy?
Not headline stuff
but still she made
the front page
toward the bottom.
Chances are
she's fallen prey
to one of those
who cruise the land
powered by fury
burying their slain
beneath a floor
or stuffing them
in dumpsters.
Some rainy spring
we may read of her
return, transformed.
Buoyed by soggy
ground, her bones
will rise, a glimmer
through the mat
of rotted leaves.
This time she will be
buried on page four
and if we think of her
at all, it will be

to wonder what went
through her mind
in that piquant tick
of time between
the knowing and
not knowing.

Under the harsh
fluorescence, the girl
tilts back on her heels
for balance, caught
between the Red Delicious
and the Yellow Grimes,
despair pooled
in her eyes; one palm
cups a perfect apple
as if she means to gauge
the weight, the other
hand clutches the cart
where a child rides
the plastic like a cowboy,
boots pummeling
the box of Tide, his mouth
contorting to shriek.
The apple drops—
too heavy, or perhaps
it was not what she
wanted, after all.

What do they dream of—
these women of a certain age
who lean, arms crossed,
on morning tables staring
into cups of coffee growing cold—

do they think of last beans
to be picked from summer's
wrecked gardens, or winter
pears waiting in bushel baskets
for frost to mellow the flesh?

Or are they remembering
the horses limned in ink on blue-
lined pages, bursting notebooks
with their heaving flanks,
their hooves striking sparks
in the dusty schoolroom?

Framed by the leaded window, she stares out
at the barren ginkgo, waits for her husband
to stride up the walk flushed by another successful
Forgive Us Our Debts Family Finance Group.
She watches her neighbor's children scuffling
on the lawn, feels the clutch of an old familiar
sorrow, thinks how often she's said it:
We've not been blessed and tells herself:
There still may be time, God willing.

In the afternoon she'll pour out tea for
Ladies of the Altar, while behind his teakwood
desk the Rector pours out sympathy as one
lost lamb or another pours out her troubled heart.
Women of the Parish wonder how it would be
married to this man of God, princely in his purple
chasuble and satin stole: *This is my body: eat.*

They imagine her with him, communion
in the sacred marriage bed—secretly they doubt
she's worthy of his flesh. She doesn't know it
yet, but deep inside her ovary a deadly cell
has split and split again to replicate itself
like loaves and fishes. Within a year her sorrow
will be gone, as sorrows finally are, as they
will be for all of us. For now, she waits, her patient
shoulders slumped, like a child who's given up
all hope of ever being first with anyone.

After the solemn reaffirmations—she, in a flurry
of pale chiffon; he, wearing the dark-blue suit
he'll be buried in—they drift from the sanctuary
to the basement of the church, to the thick white
squares of cake and pink punch waiting
in plastic goblets, to the guests assembled.

Neither turns to the other, not even when the toast
is raised. Years ago they were ravenous—
couldn't get their fill of gazing into the other's
eyes, the secret glances across a room, the shy
glimpse in lamplight of a naked body—but
by now every curve and dimple, wart, and wen
is memorized—encoded in the neurons.

No matter that this time next year will pass
unsung, that they will sit face to face
at the kitchen table while she spoons soup
into his mouth and looks into his puzzled
eyes; no matter that she will half drag,
half carry him into the bathroom and pull
his trousers down, that she will hold
him, week after week until she can
no longer bear the weight. No matter.

Let them eat their cake in celebration—
in remembrance of a pure endurance
one day after another swallowing the years
with their alarms and provocations.
Let them emerge from the doors
of the church in the last of the day
and hurry down the steps, shoulders
hunched against the stinging rain of rice.

At the end, there is always a woman
who keeps the faith, who stands
at a tub, bereft, her tears rising to blur
the traffic of churning laundry
the argyle sock dipping a toe
into the surf, a flailing pajama sleeve
waving an empty good-bye . . .

not unlike our foremothers who,
when one husband or another
was carried home from the fields
or the mine, would gather up
the softest rags and white lye soap
to scour his flesh until the water ran
gray in the basin and the nacreous
skin of his body gleamed . . .

who would, weeping, button across
the chest of even the worst of miscreants
his best linen shirt, scrubbed
with knuckles raw against the wash-
board, then boiled in a kettle
to an unsullied brightness, no less
immaculate than the robes
of martyrs or saints.

I can't remember names—except
for birds. Names ought to show
a person who you are or what
you do: mourning dove, for
instance, or rufous-sided
towhee says it all.

When Henry died I let the feeder
go but still they came, and came
again, astounded it was gone:
fifty years of millet, sunflower
seed and corn until one night
I heard his voice

as plain as day, *Why Belle, for
shame—you'd let the poor things
starve for lack of care?* And so
I kept it up 'til now. Here they got
no use for birds, wouldn't know
a myna from a moose.

For devilment I call them by
some made-up name, like Missus
Crow or Mister Razorbill to see
their feathers rise, their beaks
pull in and hear them thinking:
Senile. Daft old fool!

Some days I sit for hours in this
hard chair; I close my eyes and
let the names of birds fly round
inside my head: *northern shrike,
whip-poor-will, night-hawk,
butcher bird.*

The wily Sumac—inch by inch they creep
in camouflage, green aborigines
each year a little closer, down the steep
hill behind the house, disguised as trees.
Intrepidly, each autumn they reveal
their savage red skins glowing in the light
then slip back among the beeches to conceal
themselves once more from pale-face sight.

Sometimes in dreams I see their bare limbs gleam
their fiery tomahawks upraised for war
as one by one they slip across the stream
and storm the fortress of the kitchen door.
They mean to claim their own lost paradise.
This time beads and trinkets won't suffice.

IV

After days of thrash and thrust, of wingtips
dipping to fracture the smooth, green plate
of the pond, the drakes emerge, sleek

with iridescent arrogance, their sex-besotted
hens behind. Last May we watched, three of us
by the window; you, fresh from your third

cure, fingers locked around the coffee cup
to keep your hands from trembling as, two by
two, the mated pairs climbed the hill behind

the house to prod the shrubbery and test
grasses for a hidden nesting spot—except
for one alone, who'd somehow lost a foot

peglegging up the slope with neck outstretched
and wings unfurled for balance. Unchosen
or abandoned, she picked one pair to follow,

dogged them until they took her in, and—
if not exactly welcomed—was tolerated
like an uninvited guest who comes for lunch

and stays until Lent. All summer long she stayed
afloat, sculler with a broken oar, riding shotgun
for her adopted kin: the pair and seven young.

You cheered her on for her audacity, musing
on the fate that brought her to this odd *ménage-
à-trois*, named her Eleanor for Mrs. Roosevelt.

A year has passed, and knowing what I know
of natural law, have little hope, for winters
here are long and hard—fox and owl must eat—

but still, I scan the flock, remembering you,
how ardently you'd wished for her another season.

When winds of the past blow cold
over marked and unmarked graves
they whisper ancient quarrels,
last words spoken carelessly
or carelessly unspoken.

There comes then to the mouth
the brassy taste of unpayable,
unpaid debts—until sorrow,
the color of iron, clamps
down like the jaws of a vise.

You stand by the black window
yearning for the gold
of a rising day; you wait
for the creak of the copper
rooster in its slow hard turning.

Beneath the gray and tattered sky, the time
Of year when nature shows her brittle bones,
When trees, pale troops, assemble in the gloom
And frozen pond ice cracks—contracts—and groans,
We gathered in our spirits, as a modest girl
Will gather in her skirts, we felt the bite
Of sleet, the sting of ice, the snowy whirl—
And still held fast against December's spite.

Spring came like doom, full-blown in March, a fluke.
Tyrannic sun demanded frozen sap to rise
While earth, in labor, frazzled tangled roots,
Wrenched too soon from winter's icy vise.
Pride in perseverance was our fatal flaw—
Our hearts could not withstand the early thaw.

Nothing helps—not the laboring bellows
nor the poker prodding the flanks
of the sullen logs which grudge us less
than lukewarm light, lackluster heat.
Sold a bill of goods in August, now
we suffer through the worst of winters,
duped by the salesman glad to trade
our gullibility for a pile of useless
wood—only tempers flare; we reach
for shawls, another sweater.

Lacking the stuff from which good fires
are made—the solid-hearted hickory, oak
or walnut left to cure in measured
seasons—we climb the stairs to lie,
smoldering, beneath the layered quilts
while our stubborn, soft green
heartwood sulks, untempered in the stove.

        The bucket.
Rags. A cool blue bottle,
color of some improbable sky
like the one in Munich
that October, where the sullen
black bear hunkered, red-eyed
in a corner behind the room-
sized square of smeary glass.
I held my breath, wondering
whether mere sand and fire
could hold against some sudden
        rage.

        We begin.
Circle, counter-circle, hands
that meet and part; so many
years together we could do it
with our eyes shut tight.
Outside you point and gesture
like a man gone mad; beneath
the pressure of your palm
the old pane shivers. I imagine
possibilities: vicious shards,
underbelly of a pale forearm
a thin red bead of blood
        rising.

Early morning, the Georgia sky turning
from mauve to clotted gray.
All week long there had been something harsh
between us—the word for it not so pure
as hate: more like unloved. Unloving.

Twelve miles of silence save the slap
of tires on blacktop, and in the distance
tiers of blurred pines in their persistent
climbing of the foothills to the East Elijah Fork.

There, one road branched left, the long
safe way around, the other splitting right
with a sign like a palm upraised:
Dangerous Curves, Steep Grade Ahead.

Hungry for home—the walls of separate rooms—
we chose the crow's way, up and over,
our course erased by a cloud so dense I hung
from the window to recite aloud

the yellow hieroglyphics of the road while
your hands on the wheel followed my voice
around the hairpins to the peak; up there
on the dome, the basswood and oaks

held tight to their leaves, and the leaves,
pale stars, liquid silver dripping soundlessly
from their points; on our right, stillness and air,
the mountain holding its breath, holding us.

I think—for a moment—I wanted to say
the wrong word, imagining how it would feel
to slide over the brink, the onrushing void,
enclosed in that grayness—floating or falling.

This I remember: coasting down the last mile,
your thumb raised in the victory sign,
how you turned your face to me and smiled
as we broke into the sunlight where the town
spread itself, roof and chimney, like a banquet.

will miss the forest every time for the five-
lobed leaf, their fingers lingering over the braille
of saw-tooth border, vein, and insect gall

or can be found observing humankind within
the borders of the secret cell, the mitochondrial
life pulsing underneath a round myopic eye.

Makers and menders of watches, they hunch
over flywheels, springs and gears, knowing how
truly the minuscule can gauge a planet's girth;

will fail to recognize a friend across the street
yet know by heart an arm's curve, the amber chip
in one gray eye, the way a slow smile blooms.

That word. Once it flowed,
warm honey across our callow
tongues—now we sit
in silence—half-deaf, balding
and bifocaled—while I rub
your hands to take away the ache.
I no longer ask the question,
not because I know the answer;
the answer wouldn't matter.
You wanted me, I wanted you.
We are married; that
is that—but sometimes late
at night I feel your hand, fumbling
with the blanket, covering
my shoulders, keeping
me from the cold.

On a slab of Jurassic shale, an ovate
body, legs fine as eyelashes,
the mayfly's precise signature,
consummate, immortal.

Now its descendents, in a tumult
of mating, roil the air on Koerner's
sluggish creek below the hill
where the Ebenezer Baptist church,

its door agape, declines daily
into dust and rubble.
Beyond the church, the graveyard
encroached by nightshade

and nettle, its stones listing
or broken or gone, a few bearing
words now scarcely visible:
Eliza, Beloved Wife . . . In Perpetual . . .

A million years from now the stricken
stones will be scoured clean
and ephemerids will rise each spring
to dance above the clouded waters.

Surely not in the grave; the cargo of death
is corporal—bone and flesh—nothing,
while love must engender a critical mass,
its energy transformable—directional—
for who has never known the singular kiss
that burns the lips for decades after?

And think about two souls who meet
by chance in some familiar corner of the city;
imagine their bemusement, bombarded
by the decomposing particles we left behind.
Love's half-life lingers in a stone, a bench,
the pavements where we walked; it drifts
above the Cuyahoga, a glimmer
on the water, ash in the infinite air.

Afterword

In 1880, Wordsworth wrote a poem called, "We Are Seven," in which a little girl explains to the poet that she is one of seven siblings, though four are gone from home and two are dead. To her, they are still seven.

We—our little Greenville Poets group—are six, as we have always been, including the author of this book, Miriam Vermilya. Working together on Miriam's manuscript after her sudden death in January 1999 was not an unhappy task. We kept her with us, saying, "What would Miriam think of this? Should we put this poem back in or keep it out?" etc. There was no time in which we didn't consider her presence among us—where she remains, witty, wise, a stickler for correct grammar, young at heart.

At a reading planned for February at a local café, Miriam had decided to wear "something sparkly." She made this remark at our January meeting at her home, on the day before she died, a day in which we drank her tea and ate her cookies around the oval of her dining room table as we had so many times before. That was her bequest to us, to have shared with us the last day of her life.

She was among us as we read her poems in February along with our own, sparkling as she does in so many of these poems. She is the heartwood of our little group, and we are, as always, six.

The Greenville Poets

Selected by Robert Fink, *Heartwood* is the ninth winner of the Walt McDonald First-Book Competition in Poetry. The Competition is supported generously through donated subscriptions from *The American Scholar, The Atlantic Monthly, The Georgia Review, Gulf Coast, The Hudson Review, The Massachusetts Review, Poetry, Shenandoah,* and *The Southern Review.*